MI PIACE AIUTARE   I LOVE TO HELP

Shelley Admont
Immagini a cura di Sonal Goyal e Sumit Sakhuja

www.kidkiddos.com
Copyright©2016 by S. A. Publishing ©2017 by KidKiddos Books Ltd.
support@kidkiddos.com

All rights reserved. No part of this book may be reproduced in any form or by any electronic or mechanical means, including information storage and retrieval systems, without written permission from the publisher or author, except in the case of a reviewer, who may quote brief passages embodied in critical articles or in a review.
Second edition, 2020

Translated from English by Anna Cortese
Traduzione dall'inglese a cura di Anna Cortese

Library and Archives Canada Cataloguing in Publication
I Love to Help (Italian English Bilingual Edition)/ Shelley Admont
ISBN: 978-1-5259-2286-2 paperback
ISBN: 978-1-77268-992-1 hardcover
ISBN: 978-1-77268-990-7 eBook

Please note that the Italian and English versions of the story have been written to be as close as possible. However, in some cases they differ in order to accommodate nuances and fluidity of each language.

Per quelli che amo di più-S.A.
For those I love the most-S.A.

Jimmy saltellava intorno alla macchina, tutto emozionato. "Andiamo al mare!" gridò felice. "Andiamo al mare!"

Jimmy bounced around the car in excitement. "We're going to the beach!" he shouted happily. "We're going to the beach!"

Il papà rise, aprendo il portellone posteriore dell'auto. "Esatto!" disse, "E' una splendida giornata di sole e vogliamo partire al più presto."

Dad laughed as he opened the trunk of the car. "That's right!" he said, "It's a lovely sunny day and we want to get going quickly."

"Perché non ci aiuti a trasportare l'occorrente in macchina? I tuoi fratelli ci stanno già aiutando."

"Why don't you help us carry the things we need to the car? Your brothers are helping already."

Jimmy smise di saltellare e guardò verso il portone d'ingresso della loro casa.

Jimmy stopped bouncing and looked towards the front door of their house.

I suoi due fratelli stavano aiutando a portare il necessario alla macchina.

Jimmy's two brothers were helping carry things to the car.

Il fratello maggiore aveva tra le mani secchielli colorati e palette, mentre il fratello di mezzo stava trasportando il cestino da picnic.

The oldest brother had colorful buckets and spades in his hands, and the middle brother was carrying the picnic basket.

"Vieni, Jimmy!" lo chiamò la mamma dall'ingresso. "Tu puoi portare la sacca dei teli mare o questa piccolo sdraio. Non dovrebbe essere troppo faticoso."

"Come, Jimmy!" Mom called from the doorway. "You can carry the bag of towels or this small beach chair. It won't be very hard."

Jimmy lanciò uno sguardo ai teli mare e allo sdraio. "No, grazie!" disse con un largo sorriso. "Sono troppo impegnato a SALTELLARE!"

Jimmy looked at the towels and chair. "No, thank you!" he said with a grin. "I'm too busy JUMPING!"

Il bosco dove vivevano non era distante dalla spiaggia e Jimmy si dimenò emozionato per tutto il viaggio.

The forest where they lived was not too far from the beach and Jimmy wriggled with excitement the whole way.

Quando vide la sabbia dorata della spiaggia e la luccicante acqua azzurra del mare, cominciò a saltellare sul suo sedile.

When he saw the golden sands of the beach and the sparkling blue water of the sea, he started jumping in his seat.

"Eccoci arrivati!" disse il papà. "Usciamo e godiamoci la giornata!"

"Alright, we are here," said Dad. "Let's get out and enjoy the day!"

Jimmy scese dall'auto. "E' fantastico!" esclamò e corse giù, verso l'acqua.

Jimmy got out of the car. "This is amazing," he exclaimed and ran down towards the water.

"Aspetta!" lo chiamò la mamma. "Devi aiutarci a scaricare tutto dalla macchina."

"Wait!" Mom called after him. "You've got to help us to take everything out of the car."

Jimmy si girò, salutando con la mano la sua famiglia. "No, grazie!" disse. "Devo costruire un GIGANTESCO CASTELLO DI SABBIA!"

Jimmy turned around, waving at his family. "No, thank you!" he said. "I've got to build a GIANT SANDCASTLE!"

Corse verso un luogo adatto sulla spiaggia, proprio di fianco al mare, e cominciò a scavare nella sabbia con le mani.

He ran to a perfect spot on the beach, right next to the sea, and started to scoop sand into his hands.

Jimmy era così impegnato da non accorgersi che la sua famiglia stava facendo avanti e indietro dalla macchina, trasportando vari oggetti in spiaggia.

Jimmy was so busy having fun that he didn't notice his family going to and from the car, carrying objects down to the beach.

Nel frattempo, il castello di sabbia diventava sempre più grande.

Meanwhile, the sandcastle grew bigger and bigger.

Jimmy usò i secchielli per costruire le torri, fece un alto muro di sabbia per unirle e cominciò perfino a scavare un fossato tutto intorno, per tenere il castello al sicuro.

Jimmy used the buckets to build towers, made a great wall of sand joining them and even started digging a moat around the outside to keep the castle safe.

"Il mio castello sarà così grande che un Re e una Regina vorranno venire ad abitarci!" disse Jimmy, immaginando piccoli cavalieri e servitori correre al suo interno.

"My castle is going to be so big, a King and Queen are going to want to move in!" Jimmy said, imagining tiny knights and servants running around inside.

Mentre Jimmy stava lavorando al suo castello, i suoi fratelli maggiori andarono a caccia della più grande conchiglia che potessero trovare.

While Jimmy was working on his castle, his older brothers were hunting for the biggest shell they could find.

Il papà andò a nuotare in mare e la mamma si distese su un telo mare distante, sulla spiaggia.

Dad went swimming in the sea, looking at the fish with his snorkel, and Mom lay on a towel further up the beach.

Jimmy era così concentrato sul suo castello da non accorgersi di che cosa stesse facendo il resto della sua famiglia finché...

Jimmy was so focused on his castle that he didn't really notice what the rest of his family were doing until...

"Attento!" Jimmy sentì gridare dal papà.

"Watch out!" Jimmy heard his dad shout.

Guardò in su, giusto in tempo per vedere un'onda gigantesca avvicinarsi dietro di lui dal mare!

He looked up just in time to see a giant wave rising up beside him from the sea!

"Oh no!" gridò Jimmy quando l'onda si abbatté su di lui. Quando l'acqua si ritirò, Jimmy si distese a pancia in su, e provò a riprendere fiato.

"Oh no!" cried Jimmy as the wave crashed down on top of him. When the water pulled away, Jimmy lay on his back and tried to catch his breath.

"Puah!" Jimmy sputacchiò acqua salata e si tolse un'alga da dietro l'orecchio.

"Yuck!" Jimmy spat out salty water and pulled seaweed from behind his ears.

Poi guardò in su per vedere cosa fosse successo al suo castello.

Then he looked up to see what had happened to his castle.

"Noooo!" gridò. Il castello era completamente distrutto!

"Noooo!" he cried. The castle was completely destroyed!

Jimmy sentì calde lacrime scorrere sul suo viso mentre osservava le rovine del castello.

Jimmy felt hot tears on his face as he looked at the ruined castle.

La mamma si inginocchiò al suo fianco e lo abbracciò. Tutta la sua famiglia aveva smesso di fare quello che stava facendo e si era riunita attorno a lui.

Mom knelt down beside him and gave him a hug. All his family had stopped what they were doing and gathered around him.

"Mi dispiace per il tuo castello," disse il papà.
"I'm sorry about your castle," Dad said.

"Già, era davvero bello," disse il fratello maggiore.
"Yeah, it looked really cool," said the oldest brother.

"E grande," concordò il fratello di mezzo.
"And big," agreed the middle brother.

La mamma sorrise. Non ti preoccupare, Jimmy. Ti aiuteremo a costruirne uno nuovo."
Mom smiled. "Don't worry, Jimmy. We'll help you build a new one."

"Lo farete davvero?" chiese Jimmy.
"You will?" Jimmy asked.

"Certo!" La sua famiglia rise e si misero tutti insieme a costruire di nuovo il castello di sabbia.
"Yes!" His family laughed and they all set about building the sandcastle again.

Ma questa volta c'era qualcosa di diverso. Jimmy realizzò che con l'aiuto della sua famiglia, il castello era più grande e più bello di prima.

Something was different this time. Jimmy realized that with his family helping him, the castle was bigger and more beautiful than before.

Quando ebbero finito, era il castello di sabbia più grande che Jimmy avesse mai visto!

By the time they were finished, it was the biggest sandcastle Jimmy had ever seen!

"Guardate!" disse il fratello più grande indicando l'interno. Due granchi si erano sistemati al centro del castello. "Ha perfino un Re e una Regina!"

"Look!" the oldest brother pointed inside. Two crabs had settled down in the center of the castle. "It even has a King and Queen!"

Jimmy saltellò su e giù. Questo è il più bel castello di sempre!"

Jimmy bounced up and down. "This is the best sandcastle ever!"

Quando fu il momento di andare, la famiglia cominciò a riportare indietro gli oggetti alla macchina.

When it was time to go, the family began taking things back into the car.

Jimmy fece un grande sorriso. "Posso aiutarvi?" chiese.

Jimmy grinned. "May I help you?" he asked.

Portò i teli mare alla macchina, poi tornò indietro per aiutare a trasportare i secchielli e perfino le palette.

He took the towels to the car and then ran back to help carry the buckets and spades too.

"Wow, l'abbiamo caricato davvero in un baleno," disse il papà quando ebbero finito, guardando verso la spiaggia vuota.

"Wow, we packed that really quickly," Dad said when they were done, looking at the empty beach.

Anche quando tornarono a casa, Jimmy continuò ad aiutare, trasportando le sdraio in casa.
Even when they came home, Jimmy continued to help, carrying the beach chairs back into the house.

"Tutto funziona meglio quando ci aiutiamo l'un l'altro," disse alla mamma.
"Everything works out better when we help each other," he told Mom.

La mamma sorrise.
"Bene, ora la macchina è vuota, eccetto per una cosa."
Mom smiled. "Well, the car is empty now, except for one thing."

La mamma tirò fuori un sacchetto di biscotti. "Penso che qualcuno mi debba aiutare a mangiare questi biscotti!"
Mom pulled out a packet of cookies. "I think someone needs to help eat these cookies!"

Jimmy rise. "Si, per favore! Lo faccio io."
Jimmy laughed. "Yes, please! I'll help."

www.ingramcontent.com/pod-product-compliance
Lightning Source LLC
Chambersburg PA
CBHW061145070526
44584CB00033B/4423